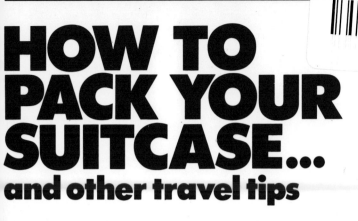

HOW TO PACK YOUR SUITCASE...
and other travel tips

Cris Evatt

Fawcett Columbine ▲ **New York**

Many thanks to Theo Gund
for her inspiration and support

A Fawcett Columbine Book
Published by Ballantine Books

Copyright © 1987 by Cris Evatt

Library of Congress Catalog Card Number: 86–91068
ISBN: 0–449–90207–2

Produced by Wink Books, Forest Knolls, California
Producer/Editor: Candice Jacobson
Book and Cover design: Charles Fuhrman
Illustrator: Edith Allgood

Manufactured in the United States of America
First Edition: April 1987
10 9 8 7 6 5 4 3 2 1

FOREWORD

Why should you buy this book? Isn't packing something everyone does fairly well? Besides, you can hang up your clothes and smooth out the wrinkles once you arrive at your destination. It doesn't matter how your suitcase looks.

I used to think the same—until I arrived in Hawaii without my favorite bathing suit—you know, the flattering one I spent weeks shopping for. Or, I shudder to remember, the time I arrived in Chicago for an important business meeting *without* the crucial brief we'd prepared to close the sale. That was before Express Mail—and before I got smart and organized.

Packing *does* matter. A disorderly, unplanned travel bag can ruin your entire trip. Picture yourself at a business meeting with a clashing tie or blouse. Or dripping in the shower when you notice there's no shampoo in your overnight bag. And how about getting caught without those prescription drugs? That's no fun when you're in a foreign country.

Get there with everything you need fresh, unwrinkled, and ready to wear. Get there looking good and trouble free. Then relax, unwind, and enjoy the adventure of being away from home.

Bon Voyage!
Cris Evatt

CONTENTS

INTRODUCTION

How do you get your clothes from your closet into your suitcase? What is your master plan? Do you end up taking two or three times more than you need? If so, then perhaps a pack mule and not this book is the answer for you.

I used to take too much, forget important items like underwear, and feel frustrated for most of the trip. What saved me was research. I spent six months in the library reading articles on packing a suitcase. I even learned how to pack five trunks like our grandparents did before airline travel.

After my reading binge, I consulted flight attendants about how to pack. Then I took some trial trips to practice what I'd learned. I became so proficient I even gave a seminar to thirty women, showing them how to pack. It was easy to get an audience because I had written *How To Organize Your Closet . . . And Your Life!* and I had an extensive mailing list from previous lectures. And the suitcase and the closet are related: The suitcase is a mini-closet.

Everything that I've learned is now in this book with step by step instructions for each traveling situation. We've included over fifty illustrations that show you exactly how to do each of the steps. (Please note that the illustrations show the shoes uncovered and patterned clothes so that you can more easily identify each item. You should still follow our advice about covering shoes and choosing mostly solid colors for traveling.) If you pay careful attention to the instructions you'll be a better packer immediately. It's easy!

I love travel. I view it as an opportunity to get away from my complex yuppie-fied lifestyle. On the road I am free of my home, yard, car (and job, if I don't bring it with me), and all of the duties these things demand. Thoreau said it all: "Our life is frittered away by detail . . . simplify, simplify."

I hope this book encourages you to travel more by making packing simpler. You may also find, after reading it, that your closet and life become more organized.

The
Organized
Traveler

Get there without a hitch. Sub-scribe to the principles of organizing. First, there's the Simplicity Principle: rid yourself of the unessential. The less you have, the less you will have to maintain. Secondly, there's the Systems Principle which states that "everything must have its place."

Sally Field is fanatical about organizing: "Yesterday, I had three scripts to read, but I was outside cleaning the garage, making sure all of the bikes were on the right hooks. It's pathetic, but I can't work if the garage isn't straightened."

I can't either. Before I pack, the basics are handled. There are no dirty dishes, unmade beds, or bills unsent. It's so much easier to think when you are in an uncluttered environment.

If you really want to get uncluttered and you have a few months before your next trip, read *Clutter's Last Stand* by Don Aslett. He inspires, cajoles, and informs you about getting your act organized.

The organized traveler isn't over-burdened with luggage. Each item has a place and is readily found. There are no misplaced belts, toiletries, or tickets. Clothing doesn't become wrinkled and outfits match.

If you normally do three out of the four steps in this chapter, then you are on your way to being an organized traveler. You merely need to refine and polish your technique. If you don't do any of the four steps regularly, then read this book twice.

FOUR PACKING STEPS

Christopher Robin in *Winnie the Pooh* said: "Organizing is what you do before you do something, so that when you do it, it's not all messed up." Below are four steps for organized packing. Done thoughtfully, they will help you reach your destination in style.
1. Make a Packing List
2. Gather Everything on the List
3. Pick Your Bags
4. Pack Right
Each step will save you time, money, and energy. Vacations and business trips are never long enough, and time away from home costs more. Steep hotel bills, transportation costs, and res-taurant tabs make traveling the most expensive time, on a per diem basis, of your life.

Step 1. Make a Packing List

People who used to travel with eight pieces of luggage made lists in order not to leave anything out. Today's travel-ers, with fewer pieces of luggage, need to make lists to keep from putting too much in.

Lists permit you to double-check, to make sure you have everything you *absolutely* need. Even the most brilliant mind cannot compete with the trusty list. You don't want to forget necessities that cost more in hotel shops—not to mention the frustration and time lost in locating them.

After making your list and referring to it for packing, carry it with you in your purse or briefcase. This way, if the air-line loses your bags, you'll have it for the insurance claim form.

Chapter Two includes a format for a packing list. Feel free to Xerox the sheet and reuse it for all your future vacations.

Step 2. Gather Everything on the List

Make your list a few days before your trip so you'll have time to ponder it. Then, the day or night before your departure, you are ready to pack.

Gather everything on the list and place the items on a bed, a table, or any flat, convenient surface. Try not to use the floor, so you'll not have to bend down. Save your back! Packing is enough of a strain without unnecessary bending.

Group everything by type: clothing, accessories, make-up, toiletries, shoes, lingerie/underwear, odds 'n ends. Most people pack as they pull items from their closets and drawers. The *new* organized you will, of course, eschew this temptation. Random packing results in last-minute panic.

Step 3. Pick Your Bags

You may have several travel bags, so you'll want to pick the right bag, or bags, for each trip. Remember, your goal is to take as few pieces as possible. Visualize everything you have laid out in only one or two bags. Below are simple options:
Underseat Carry-On
Garment Bag
Carry-On/Garment Bag
Carry-On/Standard Pullman

If your bags are worn-out or dated, you may be in the market for new luggage. See Chapter Eight for the "lowdown on luggage."

Step 4. Pack Right

The whole task of packing should take no longer than an hour or so. Turn on some lively music and make a game out of the packing process. I like the album *Footloose,* but my friend Liza goes for *Carmen.* Play whatever will make packing more enjoyable for you!

Study Chapter Four to learn the mechanics of packing (folding, rolling, and stuffing), pick a packing plan from Chapter Six, and you'll be ready to go in no time!

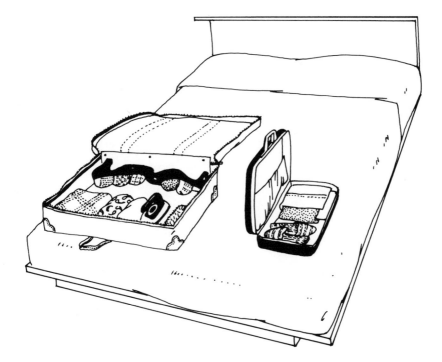

The Packing List

"The horror of that moment," the King went on, "I shall never forget it!"

"You will, though," the Queen said, "if you don't make a memorandum of it."
Jabberwocky, Stanza 6
Lewis Carroll

Several days before you pack, prepare a list of what you'll need. No doubt you'll remember your favorite suit and running shoes, but it's easy to forget some less glamorous essentials. Keep the list for future trips and change it according to your needs.

Before putting your globe-trotting attire and accessories on paper, consider the weather, your activities, local customs, travel time, and transportation mode.

Check *U.S.A. Today* and *The Weather Almanac* for the weather. Your local library has the almanac for easy reference. Weather is your most important concern.

List your activities. Will you be attending a convention, going to fine restaurants, or will you simply bask on a beach and disco in the evenings? What's your pleasure or business? Consider also the length of your trip. Will you need to launder away from home and live with less? Many experienced travelers believe that the longer the trip, the less you should pack.

What are the local customs—and taboos? Ask your travel agent. Will you be going by plane, car, train, or boat?

HOW DOES AN EXPERT MAKE A PACKING LIST?

Diane Parente is one of San Francisco's movers and shakers in the fashion consulting business. She is the founder of Successful Images, a personalized shopping and consulting service, and she is the founder of the Association of Image Consultants. Her twenty years' experience and training in fashion, image, and color analysis led me to think that Diane would be a good person to talk to about travel wardrobes. Here is what she had to say:

"The disappearance of the porter has done more than the appearance of the super jet to change our thinking about smart travel planning. The fact is, you will probably have to carry your own luggage unless you are traveling in luxury. Not much fun in itself, but what is fun is the freedom that results. We are forced into a discipline, a heavy editing of what we take.

"I find natural fabrics — silks, cottons, and wools — to be the most practical and comfortable fabrics to travel with. Silks are especially wonderful. They take up a minimum of space, look terrific, and are easy to steam out in the shower.

"With the exception of my two-piece print dress, I always travel with solid colors. I rely on attractive scarves and simple jewelry to pull an outfit together. Accessories weigh practically nothing and can fill in all the leftover spaces in a suitcase.

"Here is a basic three-week wardrobe worked around one neutral color (in this case tan, but could be any basic color)":

Day

1 raincoat, tan poplin (can serve as a robe in a pinch)
1 jacket
1 pair pants—same tan as jacket
1 skirt
1 2-piece dress, navy. Use with tan pieces.
2 shirts: creme and tan, navy stripe
3-4 t-shirts: red, navy, yellow, cream
1 pair jeans
1 navy pullover sweater
1 wrap sweater in red
1 pair walking shoes: navy and tan
1 pair evening espadrilles: navy
1 shoulder bag
1 clutch bag that can fit inside shoulder bag
Scarves, several

Evening

2 dresses in becoming colors (silk-like crepe de chine)
1 pair of evening sandals: beige

"My choice for a suitcase is one of those lightweight yet sturdy bags made of parachute fabrics. The money I save on tipping porters goes instead to midnight snacks from room service!"

MAKING YOUR OWN PACKING LIST

Try breaking your daily activities into time blocks and then figure out from that what you'll need to pack. If you project each day of your vacation in this fashion, you should be able to see how to mix and match favorite items and pack less.

For a trip to Hawaii you might list: Day 1: Morning activity is swimming. You'll need your bathing suit, coverup, and beach sandals. Put them in box one on the chart on the opposite page. Afternoon activity is sight-seeing. You'll need shorts, a sleeveless blouse, a sweatshirt, and walking shoes. Any accessories? Put them in the appropriate boxes. You don't have to put something in every box. This is just to help you think! For the disco in the evening you might want your new tube dress, strapless bra, and high-heel sandals.

For a business trip to New York in the winter, your list will look very different.

Morning
Outfit: Navy leotard, tights
Underwear: Exercise bra, white underpants
Accessories: Tennis shoes
Activity: Exercise

Afternoon
Outfit: Gray suit, pink blouse
Underwear: White bra and underpants, gray pantyhose
Accessories: Black heels, red scarf, deco earrings, white pearls, black purse
Activity: Business meetings

Evening
Outfit: Black wool Anne Klein dress, red wool coat
Underwear: Black bra and underpants, black stockings
Accessories: Black heels, black purse, diamond earrings, diamond necklace, Gucci belt
Activity: Theater

Plan each day of your trip in the same way. (Xerox our form for your convenience.) Then make a formal list like Diane Parente's. You will probably have many duplicates as you will wear the same clothes and accessories more than once. When your list is finished, make a copy of it and file it to review for future trips. Be sure to check your list as you pack and cross off each item as it goes into your bags.

THE PACKING LIST

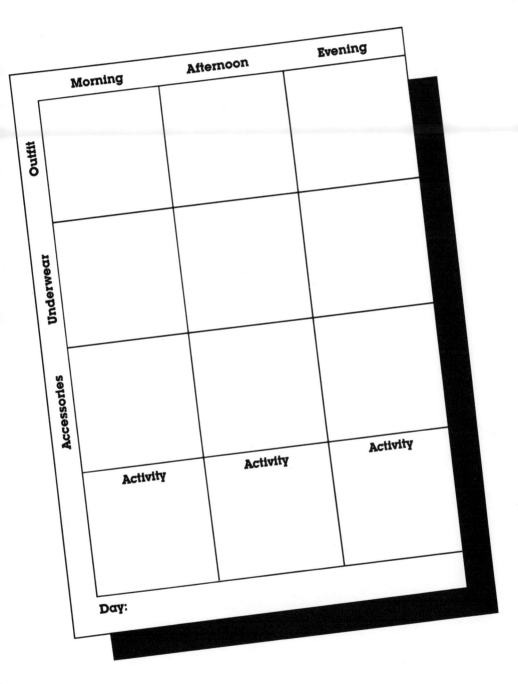

Morning · Afternoon · Evening

Outfit

Underwear

Accessories

Activity · Activity · Activity

Day:

Picking
What to
Pack

What clothes are you going to pack? Some clothes make good traveling companions while others belong home in the closet. You'll need multi-purpose, comfortable, wrinkle-proof fashions, so you can travel carefree and light. "Beware of all enterprises that require new clothes," warned Thoreau. You have plenty, too many, in your closet, already.

FASHION AXIOMS

Choose two to three basic colors. Keep your colors simple: cream and khaki, black and white, mauve and gray, navy and tan. Splash on color with ties, scarves, and shirts. Bright accessories are the only color you need.

Simple styles work best. Simple lines make for easy mixing-and-matching. Avoid faddish lengths, collars, and sleeves.

Go for solids, not patterns. Almost any solid color will go with any other solid color. Patterns are limiting! Think of paisleys, bold stripes, and flowered items as traveling extravagances.

Medium to dark tones are best. Whites and pastels are easily soiled and should be taken only if the fabric is easily hand-washable. You'll want to wear most of your clothes more than once, so choose darker tones.

Don't expect to break shoes in. Make sure your shoes are comfortable. You'll be walking more than usual, often on hilly streets and quaint cobblestones. Limit yourself to two pairs: a pair each for day and evening use. Boots are bulky and take up too much space. If you must bring them, wear them. Put some soft slippers in your carry-on to give your feet relief in flight.

Take underwear that's fun to wear. Comfort starts with underwear. Women, avoid tight girdles, hose, and bras. They get tighter and hamper circulation during long plane and car rides. Also, watch out for snug waistbands, belts, and collars.

Try the layered look. Wear layers of clothing on planes and trains and carry more. Your shoulders will thank you! Toss layers into the overhead compartment as the temperature climbs.

Esther Williams said, "Don't forget your swimsuit." How many times have you stayed in a hotel with a sign, "Heated Pool"? Weren't you miffed when you forgot your swimsuit? Don't do it again for your body's sake!

Take old clothes; discard as you go. Pack some of your soon-to-be discards. Your luggage will lighten up as you give old clothes to relatives, chambermaids, and local charities. Old underwear can be unloaded after one wearing!

FABRICS AND HOW THEY TRAVEL

Laurie Scannell, a fashion consultant from Sacramento, California, is an expert on fabrics and what happens to them when compressed snugly into luggage. What follows is information she has provided exclusively for this book:

"As a rule of thumb, synthetic fabrics tend to be more wrinkle resistant than natural fabrics. They also tend to feel hotter or clammier when worn because their quick-drying properties make them less able to absorb moisture. They are, unless used in a blend with a natural fiber, better and more comfortably worn in cool, dry climates.

"All man-made fabrics except rayon are to varying degrees heat-sensitive. Thermo-plastic (heat-sensitive) fibers can be permanently pleated by heat, an advantage. But the shape of a garment can be destroyed by too hot an iron or clothes dryer.

"Nylon and polyester are the most resilient fabrics. Fiber blends or wash and wear are also an excellent choice for travel. They are a blend of fibers, natural (e.g. cotton or wool) with a synthetic (e.g. polyester or Acrilan).

"This retains the characteristics of the natural fiber, while adding the wrinkle resistance of the synthetic. To enjoy the wrinkle-resistant character of the synthetic, be sure to have a minimum of 50% synthetic in a medium-weight or blend (wool types) and 65% synthetic in a lighter blend (cotton).

"'Durable Press' garments are a bit more tricky. They must be laundered precisely as the manufacturer instructs, unlike wash and wear clothes which return to the shape of the fabric. 'Durable Press' items are best machine

Acetate, rayon, triacetate—all members of the same family. Avoid the first two as they require dry cleaning and also wear poorly. Triacetate is a good choice; it's wrinkle resistant and launders easily.

Acrylics—resemble wool and are often blended with wool. Do not wring if hand washing. Most common trade names are Acrilan or Orlon. Wrinkle resistant, often used for very light knits, launders well.

Cotton—wrinkles in use, requires ironing.

Linen—crushes and wrinkles easily. May be finished with "Durable Press," but I'd avoid this for traveling.

Nylon—resists wrinkles and washes well, but may feel clammy and uncomfortable in warm or humid weather. Trade names include Anso, Antron, Canterce, Quiana.

Polyester—excellent to pack. Easy to launder, do not over-dry or dry clean. May be too warm to wear in hot climes. Trade names: Dacron, Fortrel.

Silk—must be dry cleaned as a rule and tends to wrinkle. Wrinkles are easily steamed out in the shower.

Wool—resilient, warm, but choose a washable type or one blended with acrylic.

washed and dried at low temperatures. They should not be wrung out or twisted, as they tend to crease and require ironing. Dry them by soaking, and hang to drip dry."

"I would avoid velvets altogether, and be careful of all napped fabric. When in doubt, simply ball up the garment or part of it, hold it a moment, then check to see how it reacted. If it's crushed-looking, leave it home. Velours of the terrycloth-knit type seem to pack well from my experience. Having your denim items professionally laundered and lightly starched will make them pack better and wear longer."

TIPS FOR TRAVELING WOMEN

Take lightweight dresses. A dress is lighter in weight, takes up less space than a suit or pantsuit, and in some countries is more socially acceptable. Pick styles that come in wash-and-wear synthetics for easy care. I like the synthetics that look like silk. Classy.

Reversibles are versatile. Stylish, reversible jackets, vests, and topcoats make two garments in one. Some jackets are flowered on one side and plain on the other. Cute.

Remember the sweater set? Do you have a cardigan with a matching crew-neck or turtle? Take it on a trip and wear it separately or together. Clever.

Add quick glamour with metallics. Bronze belts, shoes, and bags add excitement to any dress, suit, or pantsuit. Spice up an evening ensemble with a metallic camisole or tube-top. Great pick-me-ups for a tired, yet beloved, black suit.

Pack your shawl. Shawls are easy to pack and versatile. Six-foot long ponchos and simple triangles look great over a dress, turtleneck, or jacket. Belt it, if you like.

Bejeweled. Keep jewelry to a minimum and wear it. Gold is the most versatile. The ultralight traveler would wear a simple gold chain, ring (or rings), and gold earrings. If you bring additional pieces, pack them in a safe place–your purse or carry-on bag.

FOR MEN ONLY

Pack lightweight sweaters. Turtlenecks pack easily and can be worn with jackets instead of less wrinkle-resistant dress shirts and ties. Colorful Lands' End cotton crewnecks are comfortable, inexpensive, easy to wash, and they make men look dapper.

Loafers aren't just for loafing: They're great for brisk treks through unfamiliar grounds, comfortable and handsome, and a good choice in addition to the dressy black shoe.

Shoulder bags are in. Functional new shoulder bags range from Safari to briefcase styles, from leather pouches to small roll bags. All make ideal in-flight carry-alls.

Take a supply of old ties. Take several outdated and outlandish old ties and give them away as you gad about. Your bags will lighten up, leaving more room for purchases. Roll the ties or hang them over a hanger.

There are underwear options. Nylon jockey shorts are lightweight and take up less space than traditional men's underwear. Also, upcoming are paper throw-away shorts made in Taiwan that will cost about fifty cents a pair. Look for them!

Where to stash cash. Experienced travelers know how handy concealed cash is for emergencies. Take a moneybelt and survive unexpected developments.

Folding, Rolling, and Stuffing

N ow that you've picked your clothes, here are three basic ways to prepare them for a suitcase, garment bag, or duffel. Note our advice on which garments go best with each packing technique.

FOLDING

Every fold is a potential crease. Clothes should be folded, so that if sharp creases appear, they will emphasize, as much as possible, the structural lines of your garment. Make sure that good, clean edges and corners are made. Avoid folds at corners that can cause short, diagonal creases. Fold your clothes on a flat surface–your bed or a table–and fold everything *before* loading your suitcase.

I have discovered two efficient folding methods. Use the one that works best for you. Try both!

Basic folding

The clothes that will cause the most grief and wrinkle the easiest are shirts, some sweaters, skirts, pants, jackets, and dresses. No need to worry about underwear, t-shirts, slinky nightgowns, casual sweaters, and jeans. They can be rolled, and I'll explain just how to do it in the next section. Now for folding instructions!

Shirts/Blouses. First, button the shirt. At the very least, button the middle button. Next, place it face down on a flat surface. Fold both sleeves in–keep them hanging down vertically–as shown in the diagram. Finally, depending on the length of the shirt, fold once at the waist, or twice, at the bottom and then at the waist.

To this method, you can add a rectangle of tissue across the back of the shirt, and some crumpled paper at the col-

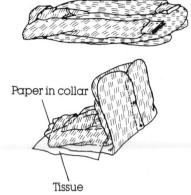

Paper in collar

Tissue

lar. Place the shirt in a plastic bag for further protection. Silk blouses adore this special treatment!

Sweaters. Most people (and clothing stores) fold sweaters like shirts. I find this time consuming, creating a bulky bundle. For a faster, flatter method, try these simple steps:
1. Place the sweater face down on a flat surface.
2. Fold one sleeve and then the other across the back, *horizontally.*
3. Fold in half, bringing the bottom of the sweater to the shoulders.
4. Lay facing upward in your suitcase. Heavy sweaters don't benefit from the use of tissue, whereas light ones do. Plastic bags are great for keeping delicate sweaters safe and tidy when you rummage through your suitcase.

If the sweater has a turtleneck, begin by flapping the neck toward the back before folding the sleeves.

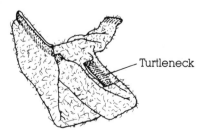

Turtleneck

Jackets/Blazers. There are a half-dozen ways to fold a jacket. I have chosen two that work well for me. The techniques are simple, requiring few folds. Give them both a try before your next Himalayan trek.

Folding a jacket for a standard suitcase.

1. Lay the jacket face up, making sure that the shoulders are squared and the collar flat.
2. Fold both arms across the jacket horizontally. Keep the armholes as flat as possible. The jacket will look like it's hugging itself.
3. Now fold the jacket in half, bringing the bottom up to the shoulders. This technique is good for jackets of all fabrics and sizes.

Folding a Jacket for a duffel, backpack, soft suitcase.

The main trick is to fold it from the inside out.

1. Lay the jacket flat, lining side down. Turn the collar up and flatten.
2. Fold back the sides, so the edges nearly meet at the center seam.
3. Fold the jacket in half on the center seam. Then fold at the waist for an even smaller package.

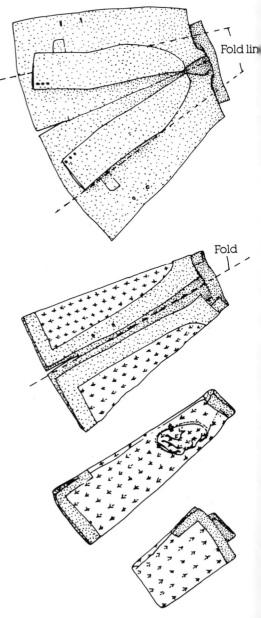

Fold line

Fold

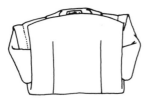

Skirts. Regardless of the skirt shape, you'll want to fold it into a neat rectangle to fit into your suitcase. It is important to use tissue to prevent creases. Denim and crinkly cotton skirts are an exception.

1. Lay the skirt face down and smooth. Place some tissue paper in the center.
2. Fold both sides of the skirt a third of the way in, making straight vertical lines from the waist.
3. Don't fold near the hemline. Make a horizontal fold close to the waist, because a crease close to the hemline is more noticeable. How small you fold a skirt depends on the size of your suitcase.

Pants. Pants should be hung in the closet with all four seams matched up, making a crease down the center of each leg. It doesn't matter whether you hang pants by the waist, cuffs, or over a hanger.

1. Lie the trousers flat lengthwise. Smooth.
2. Fold the pant legs between the knee and cuff.
3. Fold again, bringing the first fold up to the waist. Never fold pants at the knee. A crease there would be noticed and not an indicator of successful dressing.

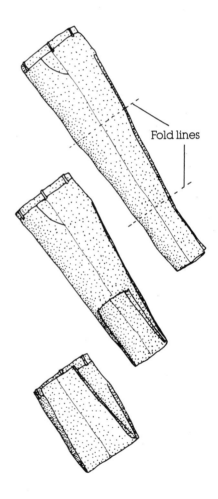

Fold lines

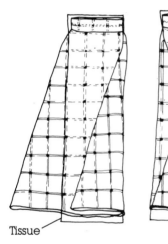

Tissue

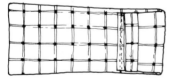

Dresses. The top half of a dress is folded like a blouse, while the bottom half is folded like a skirt. If your dress has buttons, fasten them before you begin.

1. Lay the dress face down and smooth. Place tissue paper down the center.
2. Fold one side a third of the way, forming a straight line.
3. Fold the sleeve down vertically.
4. Repeat steps 2 and 3 on the opposite side.
5. Now fold the skirt at the bottom several inches up from the hem.
6. Fold the dress at the waist. Your previous fold should end up at the top of the shoulders.

Always pack your dresses face up. You may insert them in a plastic bag for added protection. Use more tissue when packing a silk dress or a very fragile one. You may also stuff the sleeves with loosely crumpled tissue.

Cinderella would have packed her ball gown this way. It's not that complex.

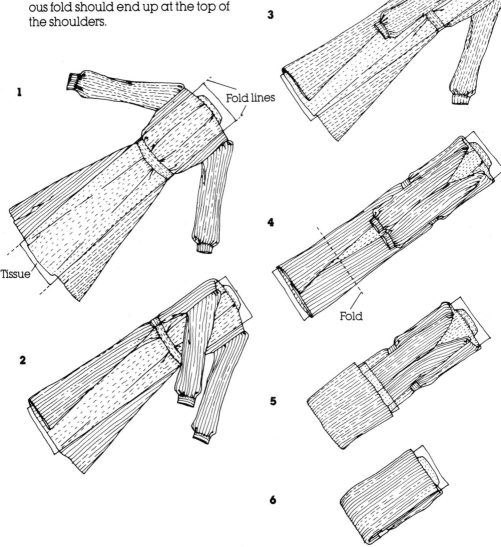

Fold lines

Tissue

Fold

22

Interfolding

The fastest, most wrinkle-proof way to pack is to interfold. Flight attendants frequently use this method, which is unknown to most travelers. Interfolding lets each garment pad another at a crucial fold line. Long items—slacks, dresses, skirts—are laid out first, alternating horizontally. Shorter items—sweaters, shirts, jackets—are laid vertically.

The top of each garment (face down, sleeves inward and straight) sits against a suitcase edge, while the bottom half hangs over the side. Lay out as many items as you like, depending on the size of your bag.

After the garments are placed, flip the ends into the suitcase. Alternate, so each fold is cushioned by another item. You will end up with a rectangular pile of clothes securely held together. It is easy to pick up the whole pile at once!

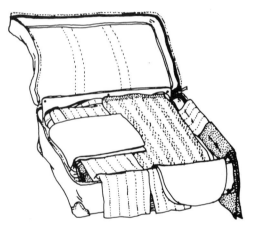

When you arrive at your destination, unfold your clothes and let them hang out of the suitcase. Hanging them up is optional. To get to an item in the center of the pile, insert one hand, lift up the clothes on top of it. Remove the item with your other hand. After wearing a garment, place it on top of the pile.

ROLLING

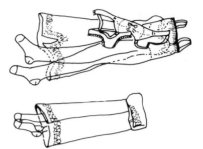

Rolling right along! But first, a word of warning. Not every garment that can be rolled should be. Rolling is mainly an alternative for casual clothes, nightwear, underwear, accessories, and wrinkle-resistant synthetics. For a complete list of packables and their rollability, read on!

Trousers. Lay your pants on a flat, firm surface. Roll them tightly, starting from the bottom. Sporty trousers, especially jeans, can be rolled up with a t-shirt and underwear inside.

Nightwear. Place face down and then fold lengthwise in thirds. Roll up firmly from the bottom. To make a set: Place a nightgown or p.j.'s down the center of the back of the robe before rolling.

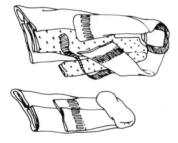

Underwear. Great for rolling in sets! Men, put an undershirt, shorts, and socks together. Women, combine a slip folded in thirds lengthwise with pantyhose, bra, and panties.

Accessories. Belts, ties, and scarves are all very easy to roll.

Socks, pantyhose. Most people know how to roll up socks. If you don't ask your mother!

Skirts. Pleated and knit skirts come out nicely when rolled. It's not good, however, to roll most skirts unless you pad the center with a rectangle of tissue and roll carefully.

Dresses. Only dresses made out of crinkly Indian cotton and crushproof synthetics can be rolled. Fold most dresses.

Bathing suit, beach towel, robe, and rubber thongs. Roll your beach ensemble together with the towel on the bottom. Thongs can go in a Baggie. I'd rather be in Tahiti, too!

Casual shirts. Polo's, t-shirts, and flannels all roll nicely. Fold in thirds lengthwise, then roll from the bottom. Don't roll dress and business shirts.

Casual jackets. Windbreaker, down, and denim jackets roll without wrinkling noticeably. Roll them as you would a shirt. *Fold* suit jackets!

Sweaters. Most sweaters roll nicely, especially lighter weight ones. Bulky sweaters are difficult to do and come unrolled easily. Lightweight turtlenecks can be placed on top of a pair of Levis and then rolled. Neat combo!

Coats. Forget it! Coats rarely come out of a roll gracefully.

Tip: Cushion folded clothes with rolled ones. Soft rolls can fill in gaps around the outside edges of your suitcase, and can cushion folds of fragile fashions. Tightly rolled slips, undies, nightgowns, and t-shirts can be placed at the fold lines of dress slacks, silk shirts, blazers, and skirts. Try this idea on your next trip!

STUFFING

Stuffing your clothes isn't better than folding or rolling. It's different. And it's a great space-saving method.

Stuff some items into others: Empty shoes can be stuffed with rolled-up socks or a secret bag of jewelry. Sleeves can be stuffed with rolled slips to keep from wrinkling. Stuff a knit hat with gloves or a woolen scarf when you go to Moscow. Are you starting to get the idea? If you wear a trench coat to the airport, stuff the pockets with small items. Don't waste empty spaces.

Stuff clothes into hose: Now for a tried-and-tested trick for women invented by flight attendants (when they were called stewardesses). Cut the top and feet off a pair of pantyhose. Fill the stretchy tubes with robes, tops, skirts, etc. Experiment with all of your crush-resistant garments. Donna Walters, a marketing assistant for American Airlines, fills her luggage with more than ten tubes of clothing, which she affectionately calls "snakes."

How to stuff: to slip the hose tube over a garment, start from the top and pull the hose down over it. You may need one whole tube, half a tube—cut the tube to fit—or two tubes for longer garments. If you need two stocking lengths, pull the first one down to the bottom of your dress or robe, then pull the second one down to meet the first. It's easy to slip hosiery over clothing. I know it sounds bizarre!

Stuffing your clothes into hose is a compact way to carry light, airy, yet bulky items that normally fill up far too much space. Garments can be arranged and rearranged in a suitcase without coming unfolded or unrolled. And you can tie a knot at the end of a piece of hose if you want to make a small, thin bag.

Clothes in tubes survive trips amazingly well. They *never* get a horizontal crease.

Wrinkle-Proof Traveling

5

Can you arrive at your destination unruffled, unwrinkled, and uncrushed? No matter how long your trip, how good you look once you arrive will depend on how well you packed. Below are ways to avoid wrinkles and preserve creases.

EIGHT WAYS TO KISS WRINKLES GOODBYE

1. Distribute weight evenly. With less slipping and sliding, you will have less wrinkling. Also, a well-balanced bag is easier to carry.

2. Pack tightly. Don't overpack! On the other hand, loose packing shifts, causing wrinkles. Fill in gaps, lumps, and corners.

3. Pack in solitude. You'll find you pack better if you are not distracted by a friend's latest gossip or grand money-making scheme.

4. Avoid damaging juxtaposition of colors and hardware. Don't put a fuzzy white sweater against black slacks, or metal against impressionable or break-able materials.

5. Cushion fragile fabrics with tissue paper. Use twisted and crushed tissue, as well as sheets formed into rectangu-lar shapes. Stuff crushed paper into sleeves. Support the back center of dresses, shirts, and skirts with flat pieces. In general, put tissue at potential wrinkle lines. (Note: Some people don't like packing with tissue because it is time-consuming.)

6. Fold and roll clothes properly. Prac-tice the methods in Chapter Four, so creases appear in the least noticeable places. For instance, it is better to fold a skirt near the waist than the hem.

7. Stuff soft clothing into folds. Use small items—socks, undies, nightgowns or p.j.'s, scarves—to stuff into folds of jack-ets, slacks, shirts, and dresses. Gently wrap a delicate silk blouse around a soft negligee.

8. Pack in plastic bags. Plastic holds air, softening creases. Use dry-cleaning bags to slip over large garments before folding. Keep the wire hangers for easy hanging. Wastebasket liners are the right size for shirts and sweaters. Sandwich bags are great for smaller items. Beware: Plastic bags melt and collect humidity in tropical climates!

IT COULDN'T BE HELPED

If, in spite of your most conscientious packing methods, a few wrinkles sneak in anyway, try hanging your clothes on the back of the hotel's bathroom door and taking a steamy shower. This will usually get rid of wrinkles in 15 to 20 minutes. Another favorite wrinkle-removing technique is to put your skirt or trousers in between two mattresses and sleep on them. In the morning your "body press" has restored their smooth-ness. Finally, if you must travel with an iron, buy a special travel iron. It has a dual voltage system for foreign travel and will fold compactly in your bag-gage. Don't rely on your hotel to supply an iron; you'll be disappointed more often than not.

Eight Packing Plans

6

I t's time to make your clothes fit the case! What follows are eight commonsense packing plans for loading several kinds of travel bags. Although it is true that no one particular plan, or set of plans, may meet *all* your needs, if some kind of plan is followed, packing is easier.

PACKING PLAN NUMBER 1:
The standard Pullman

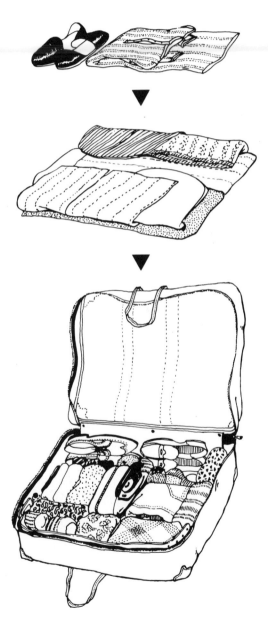

You'd like to become an excellent packer? First, master the Pullman suitcase—the simple, box-like case with a lid hinged to it. An old-fashioned technique of packing in three layers works well for both large and small Pullmans.

Bottom layer: Place heavy, irregularly shaped articles and soft rollables on the bottom. Shoes (in shoe mitts) go in first, against the hinge side. When your suitcase is standing, the weight of the shoes will not rest on clothing.

Place belts next to the rim near the handles. Next, put in the remaining bulkies—toiletries, handbag, iron, mouse traps, flashlight, camera, kitchen sink. (Are you still traveling light?) Finally, your rolled-up clothes will serve as fillers around the heavier items. Make the bottom as flat and even as possible. Balance this layer, too.

Middle layer: After you've buttoned and zipped your clothing, use the interfolding method. Pack the heavier garments first, then the fragile ones. This layer will consist of pants, skirts, dresses, shirts, and jackets.

Top layer: Place anything on top that you'll need when you first arrive in your hotel room. Your nightwear and slippers should be handy!

PACKING PLAN NUMBER 2:
The Pullman with dry cleaners' bags

Clothing hanging in cleaners' bags is a boon to the traveler. The plastic softens creases by capturing pockets of air. True, the bags are space wasters, but the lost space is traded for less wrinkling.

Bottom layer: Follow the instructions in the previous packing plan.

Middle layer: Layer your nightwear over the bottom layer.

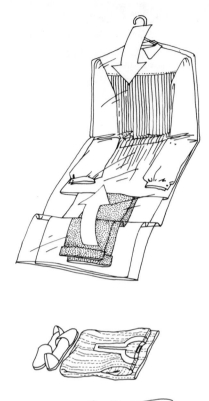

Top layer: Grab the hangers of dresses, shirts, skirts, pants, and jackets, each in a long plastic bag. Place the clothes in the suitcase lengthwise with the hangers extending on one side and the hems on the other. Next, fold the hanger side over and cover with the hem side. The clothes will be in thirds. (You may also use an accordion fold for this bundle.)

When you arrive in your hotel room, grasp the hangers, shake out the clothes, and hang them up. Immediately!

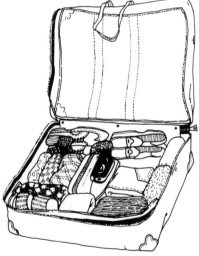

PACKING PLAN NUMBER 3:
The two-compartment Pullman

This suitcase is popular because it opens up flat, organizing clothing into two separate compartments. A sturdy flap of material fastens against the lid section. Many flight attendants prefer this case to the standard Pullman.

Side one: Pack this side as you would the bottom of the standard Pullman. Place your shoes first and then belts around the opposite rim. Next, add heavy items and soft rolled ones. Fold nightwear and place on the top of this layer.

Side two: Place clothing—trousers, dresses, skirts, shirts, jackets—in the lid section. Use the interfolding method to keep clothes as wrinkle free as possible. Always place your pants first as they are the stiffest and often longest garments. They will create a good foundation for your other clothes.

This type of suitcase is found mainly in hard-sided luggage. The soft-sided cases have zippered side compartments for organizing.

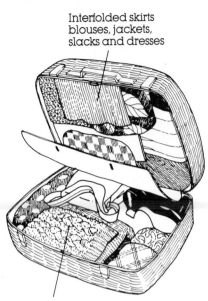

Interfolded skirts blouses, jackets, slacks and dresses

Shoes, bags, heavy bulky items and soft, rolled items

Interfolded suits and slacks

Shoes, skirts, sweaters, and toiletries

PACKING PLAN NUMBER 4:
The hanging bag

The hanging bag saves time! You don't have to check it in or pick it up from a baggage carousel. Packing and repacking is easy because many items can be hung. Many business men and women favor this bag over all others.

Hanging bags come with from zero to six coat hangers, and you can buy more. Some feature staggered hanger bars which cut down on wrinkling at the shoulders. The bags come with up to nine zippered and snapped pouches.

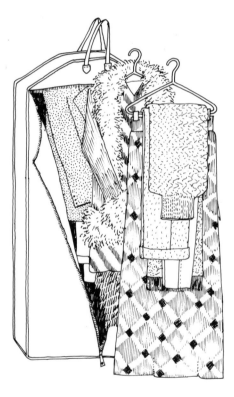

Packing it: Layer from two to four garments on a single sturdy hanger. Place garments that easily wrinkle at the back of the bag, so the fold will be less intense when the case is folded in half. At your destination, immediately place your most important garments on individual hangers in the closet to revive their shapes.

Carefully center suits, dresses, jackets, pants, and shirts before hanging in your bag. Hang sleeves a little in front of jackets, dresses, and shirts. Plastic bags, long ones, work well over these clothes, minimizing creases.

Disadvantages: Don't fill your garment bag too full or you will need a luggage cart. It can get heavy. If you transfer planes and have a long wait, you will have to schlepp it to coffee shops, magazine counters, restrooms, and phones. Not fun! Finally, there may not be room to hang your bag on the plane.

PACKING PLAN NUMBER 5:
The rectangular duffel

The duffel bag is great for short trips—sport vacations, casual overnights, and weekend trips. I take mine to Tahoe when I go skiing. The duffel comes in many shapes, sizes, and materials.

You can jump on a plane without standing in overcrowded baggage check-in lines. Duffels can be stored under your seat.

Packing it: Pack your duffel the way sailors do. Roll your clothing tightly, starting from the bottom.

First, put heavy, bulky items on the bottom of the bag. Place rolled items in an orderly fashion on top of these. Fragile items are placed in the middle of the bag, cushioned with soft rolls of clothing.

Create sets of underwear and socks in rolls, and place them in one medium plastic bag. You don't want these small items roaming all over!

Bring a large plastic bag for your soiled laundry. For a long trip include detergent in small packets or Baggies.

College students and vagabonds ("The vagabond, when rich, is called a tourist."—Paul Richard) find the casual duffel all they need for a two-month trip through Europe.

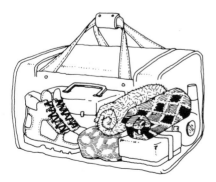

PACKING PLAN NUMBER 6:
The round duffel

The round duffel is trickier to pack than the rectangular duffel or a suitcase. It has a narrow zipper opening and elongated shape. It's hard to get into! Also, if it is not packed firmly and totally filled out, it will look lumpy. Below is a unique packing plan that will make you glad you own a duffel.

Packing it: Try the Towel Method! Place a bath towel on a bed or large table. All of your clothing will be placed on it, starting with the longest items first. Lay out your pants, then stagger your shorter garments—shirts, shorts, underwear—on top of the pants. Make sure the clothes are smoothed out and distributed evenly on the towel. Everything will be flat. Finally, roll up the towel and put it in the duffel.

Stash your shoes at the ends to lend rigidity to the bag. Put other heavy, odd-shaped items at the ends, too.

The Towel Method is ingenious because your clothes will not slip around and get wrinkled. Experiment with this plan and the one on the previous page before you book a flight for the trendy Club Med in Guaymas, Mexico.

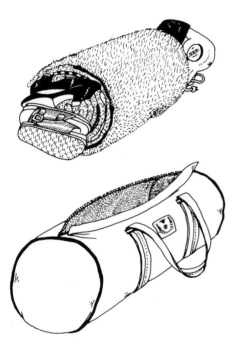

PACKING PLAN NUMBER 7:
The three-partitioned suitcase

Suitcases divided into three partitions usually come in nylon with zippers. This suitcase is becoming more and more popular because you can slip the twenty-one inch model under an airplane seat. Business women and men often use this bag along with a hanging bag—a great way to travel light!

Packing it: Packing is easiest if all three compartments open up flat.

Side one: Folded clothes go here. These clothes may be put in plastic bags for neatness.

Side two: Interfolded items go on this side. Use tie-tapes, if they are available, to hold clothes against the case. In fact, it's best to buy a three-partitioned bag with tapes in every section.

Side three: Pack the middle section like the bottom of the standard Pullman. See the illustration in Packing Plan Number 1. Put all of your bulky and rolled items in this division. It's the deepest and can handle your shoes.

The divided suitcase offers a seasoned traveler an opportunity to be highly organized. Keep in mind that ultimately you must create your own packing plans, using the ones in this book only as a guide.

Packing the three-partitioned suitcase:

Basic folded items go here! May be put in plastic bags for neatness.	Heavy, bulky and soft rolled items can go in the middle, or deepest compartment.	Interfolded items should go on the opposite side.
▼	▼	▼

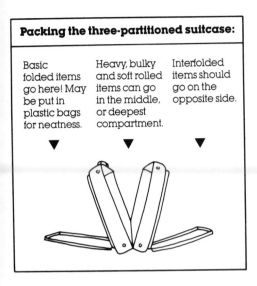

PACKING PLAN NUMBER 8:
The carry-on bag

What if your bags are lost or delayed? Are you prepared? Experienced travelers supplement checked-in luggage with a carry-on tote packed with essentials. Emergency totes come in many styles and have one thing in common: They are not larger than forty-five inches in overall dimensions, so they can be put under an airplane seat.

What to pack: You will need just one of each clothing essential. Your lost bag will, hopefully, turn up in 24 hours. If not, go shopping or to the laundromat for fresh clothing. (You will need just a new pair of shorts and a tank top in Fatu Hiva.) Use my lists as guides:

For men: Dopp Kit, one pair of underwear and socks, nightwear, one shirt, one tie (if needed), all jewelry not worn, travelers checks, business papers, camera. Businessmen often use a compartment in an attache case to carry emergency items. A laundered and folded shirt fits comfortably in most briefcases.

For women: Cosmetic kit, hair dryer, toiletries, lingerie for a day, one pair of hose, one blouse/top, nightgown, accessories (if needed), all jewelry not worn, travelers checks, business papers, camera.

The tote bag is also convenient for overnight side-trips that may lead you temporarily away from a big city destination!

What to
Pack for
the Kids

I f you are traveling with children your packing needs will increase exponentially. A little careful planning will make the difference between the thrill of a lifetime and one long nightmare. Here are some important things to remember:

TRAVELING WITH AN INFANT

What did parents do before the disposable diaper? They probably took a staff with them or stayed home. Now, with couples having fewer children and more money, there are infants who have more passport stamps before their first birthdays than the rest of us get in a lifetime. If you do decide to travel with your infant, you should plan even more carefully in order to make sure you'll have everything you need.

Plan for a messy baby! At least two changes of clothing, extra diapers, clean-up supplies, and changing sheets should be in a carry-on bag even for a short flight.

A few extra bottles (plastic, of course) are essential for long flights. Do not rely on the airline to have juices or warm milk for you.

Be sure to pack enough changes for the baby so that you don't spend your whole trip hand washing. How about buying second-hand baby clothes and leaving them behind as you travel?

Be sure to tell the airline that you will be traveling with an infant. Some airlines are nicer about babies than others—ask your travel agent for some tips.

THE OLDER CHILD

Dress your child in casual play clothes for traveling, loose-fitting garments that he can nap and lounge in comfortably and, above all, manage easily when

---

Here is a baby checklist; you'll have your own items to add:

Food (don't pack glass jars!)	Disposable diapers
Juice	Several clean cloth diapers for burping
Formula	
Spoon	
Bib	Rattle
Teether	Favorite toy
Lots of plastic bags	First-aid supplies
	Baby powder, oil
Changing sheet	Moist towelettes
Pacifier	Socket plugs for hotel room
Changes of clothes	

---

he goes to the lavatory. Flight attendants are encouraged to give children extra attention, but are often hampered because of other duties. Take along a small duffel bag full of entertaining things to do. Below is a list of ideas mothers and fathers have kindly shared with me:

1. Encourage your child to write about her plane trip to a favorite friend or relative. Some airlines supply free picture postcards of the plane and most offer free stationery.

2. Bring along a book about the American city or foreign country you will be visiting.

3. Bring along your child's favorite toy. This familiar object will give him a sense of security.

4. Teach your child a new card game. Has she ever tried "Uno"? It is simple to learn and fun to play. There is also "War" and "Fish," which may be played with a conventional deck of cards. Endure a hundred games of "Tic-tac-toe."

5. Give your child a bag full of surprises he can open on the plane. A love note from Mommy is especially comforting to a young child traveling alone for the first time.

The Lowdown on Luggage

8

Thinking about packing plans and making lists may make you realize that you need to shop for new luggage. What are your luggage needs? Do you need gear that will travel well by car, plane, train, or motorcycle? Are your trips mainly for business or pleasure?

Luggage departments have an ever-changing supply of fashionable new travel bags. There are brazen new colors, fabrics, and styles. Do you hanker for foreign, designer, or parachute bags? And how do you know if your choice will withstand the traumas of airport handling?

Before you tackle the baggage selections at your local department or specialty store, consider the following:

HOW IS IT CONSTRUCTED?

Soft-sided bags are the most popular and account for more than 90% of luggage sales. The lightweight, flexible bags come both framed and frameless. The framed cases are more practical because they can better accommodate business suits and a greater variety of clothing. The frameless bags, especially the duffel types, are best for casual overnights and sports vacations.

Hard-sided suitcases are sturdy, but unpopular. Retailers claim that their customers want to travel lighter. Molded Pullmans weigh from eight to ten pounds. In some molded cases, liquid plastic is cast in a mold, and the plastic serves as both frame and covering. In others, a plastic is molded over a wooden or metal shell. The shell itself may be molded of materials such as cellulose fiber, resins, or fiberglass, then laminated with plastic.

THE COVER STORY

Luggage can be covered with vinyl, canvas, aluminum, nylon, rayon, tapestries, leather, fiberglass, rubber, and plastic, and the list is expanding.

Canvas: Popular and practical for soft luggage. It is sturdy, waterproofable, washable, and can be easily glued or stitched if it rips.

Vinyl: Non-scuff, inexpensive, washable, and harder to repair than canvas. Corfam, according to some retailers, tends to warp and is not scratch-proof.

Nylon: The most popular material for super-lightweight bags. The higher the denier (weight), the more durable the fiber —a thousand denier is much stronger than two-hundred denier. Nylon is more resistant to tearing than plastic coverings, which are more scuff-resistant.

Urethane: Often mistaken for leather, which is more expensive. A lightweight covering, useful for carry-ons.

Cordura: The look of canvas and the superior strength of nylon. Higher resistance to tearing and abrasion than vinyl. Polyurethanes and ABS (acrylinotrile-butadiene-styrene): Used for hard-sided luggage. These tough, molded materials are usually scuff-resistant.

Acetate: Common suitcase lining. Susceptible to damage from nail polish and remover, so make sure the caps are on tight! Lining can snag and separate from the shell.

BRANDS AND PRICES

Don't buy luggage on the basis of price alone! A flood of cheap luggage is streaming into the U.S. market, and many so-called bargains don't survive one plane flight. Also, beware of outrageously priced luggage. Imagine your sadness at seeing it scuffed! Below are some reputable brands of bags:

Low-priced luggage: Sears, Penney's, Gateway, Lancer, Verdi, Le Sportsac, L.L. Bean, Lands' End.
Moderately priced luggage: American Tourister, Hartmann, Ventura, Samsonite, Skyway, Andiamo, Florentine, Athalon, Wings, Lark, Verdi, Pegasus, Land, John Weitz.
High priced luggage: Louis Vuitton, Mark Cross, Caracciola, French Company, Gucci, Halliburton, Hartmann.

COLOR CONSIDERATIONS

Neutral colors are by far the most popular. They are compatible with trench coats, purses, attache cases, shoes, and other accessories. Tan is the most sought-after neutral, followed by navy, black, and brown. Burgundy is a new basic color in luggage that goes with almost everything. If neutrals bore you, soft-sided bags come in a dazzling array of colors: Skipper Blue, Cactus Green, Geranium Red, Mellow Yellow, and Royal Purple.

THE LUGGAGE TEST

Here's a checklist you can take along when you shop for traveling gear. Give your favorite bags the touch test.

The frame: Is it resilient and strong? Stand a soft-sided, framed suitcase on the floor with the handle up. Press down lightly on the top, then release. If the frame returns to its original shape slowly, then an inferior metal may have been used.
Weight: Is it too heavy or too light for your needs? Lift it.
Handles: Are they securely attached and comfortable for carrying? How do they feel?
Lid: Does it fit properly? Do the zippers and latches work easily? Is it sturdy? Open and close the bag several times to find out.

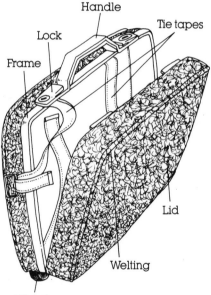

Handle
Tie tapes
Lock
Frame
Lid
Welting
Wheel

Wheels: Do they roll along smoothly? Are they well constructed? Pull the suitcase around the shop.

Lining: Does it fit properly? Tug on it to see if the seams are snug. Make sure the stitching is either double- or lock-stitching, not chain-stitching, which can unravel.

Welting: The exterior covering that protects the joints and seams from exposure must be abundant and attached firmly. Welting keeps dirt and dampness out. Check it!

Tie Tapes: Excellent for holding your clothing in place. Are they featured? Pockets and partitions: How many compartments do you need? How many are there? Feel the quality. Access: Can you get clothing in and out easily? Too much rummaging causes frustration—and wrinkles! This is the most important consideration of all.

DEALING WITH WHEELS

Departures and arrivals often include long treks through terminals and parking garages. Heavy suitcases equipped with wheels are a lifesaver. There are four ways to roll along:

1. Four-wheeled suitcases: Four small wheels come on some Pullman pieces. Make sure the suitcase comes with a handy leather or plastic pull-strap. Test the wheels on both carpeting and hard surfaces.

2. Two-wheeled suitcases: A.K.A. the cartwheel. A metal handle, tucked into the side opposite the two wheels, lifts up. The case then tilts at a forty-five-degree angle.

3. The luggage cart: You can carry several bags at once (if you're not traveling light!). Carts come with large or small wheels. Choose the larger ones! They falter less over curbs and bumps. Sturdier models can lift up to two-hundred pounds of luggage. The airlines don't check in carts because they are not liable for damaging them, sometimes a disadvantage.

4. Screw-on wheels: Larger wheels than the ones that come attached to luggage. Come in a kit that costs more than twenty-five dollars. Cannot be attached to all luggage. Not a good option.

Warning: Be careful when your wheeled luggage approaches curbs or escalators. The wheels can balk, causing your load to tip over. And don't get gravel into the wheels' mechanism. It could result in a costly repair problem.

Marking Your Luggage

Airlines load and unload about 450 million pieces of luggage each year, and, unfortunately, some of that luggage is lost, delayed, and damaged. It is estimated that nearly one-third of the complaints that passenger-relations departments receive concern mishandled baggage. Keep in mind—as the airlines like to stress—problems are relatively rare in proportion to the number of passengers carried.

HOW NOT TO LOSE YOUR LUGGAGE

Airline employees misread tags, mistag bags, set luggage aside and forget it, or haul it out of the cargo hold before it reaches its intended destination. On the other hand, in about 50 percent of the cases, passengers themselves are to blame for lost luggage. Below are some of the most useful ways you can assist airlines in handling luggage. Identify your bags in four ways. Make sure your bags are properly tagged for your own protection:

1. Name-tag the outside. Use a leather or plastic tag holder. Avoid stick-on labels. They may fall off. Write in your name, permanent or business address, and phone number.
Tip: Would-be burglars occasionally mingle in airport lines to check the names and addresses of people going on vacation. Use a business address if you possibly can.
2. Name-tag the inside. Tape an I.D. to the inside of your suitcase. Use your business card, if you have one.
3. Tape an itinerary card inside. Include the cities you plan to visit, the dates you will be in each city, and where you can be reached at each stop. If a bag is temporarily lost and then recovered, it can be quickly forwarded to the right place.
4. Add a personal marking. Many travel experts suggest distinguishing your baggage from that of others by marking it with brightly colored tape, yarn, paint, tassels, or bumper stickers.

A small symbol or wrapped handle will do. Luggage straps also serve as markers.
Tip: Recently a new product called "The Luggage Spotter & I.D. Tag" was seen at a department store chain, selling for less than two dollars. These smart-looking tags come in colorful shapes: pink hearts, red apples, golf greens, geometric shapes, balloons, and tennis racquets—all easy to spot.

Remove old baggage tags. Don't be a tag collector. (Save postcards instead.) A baggage handler can be confused by the presence of several routing tags. Failure to remove old destination tags is the number one cause of lost luggage.

Carry-on your essentials and valuables. A man can tuck a clean shirt, a razor, and important papers in his briefcase. A woman should carry make-up, a change of lingerie, her jewelry, and one outfit in a tote or underseat bag. Think of carry-on items as *lost luggage insurance.*

Finally, try to arrive at the airport at least 45 minutes before your flight. Double check your claim checks to verify that you receive one for each of your bags and that the destination marked is correct.

WHAT TO DO ABOUT DELAYED BAGS

If you and your bags do not connect at your destination, don't get hysterical. Most airlines have very sophisticated systems that (they claim) can track down about 98% of the suitcases misplaced, and return them to their proper owners within hours. If your bags do not come smoothly off the conveyor belt, report the problem to the Baggage Services Representative *before* you leave the airport. He or she will ask you to fill out a form describing your bag. Keep a copy!

On the
Road

N ow that you've packed sensibly and will arrive at your destination with the appropriate clothes for each occasion, relax and have a wonderful trip. To make your trip even better you might want to take a few tips from this chapter. I've been collecting travel tips for more than fifteen years, and these are the best of the bunch. If you come by a handy hint on your vacation, send it along to me—I'd love to hear from you. My tips are in categories:

MAILING TIPS

1. Let the shop ship it. If you buy from a reputable store, let the management send your purchase to your home. Don't schlepp it.
2. Address several manila envelopes, the 8" x 10" size, to yourself and fill them full of postcards, museum brochures, menus, small souvenirs, tax receipts, and used maps when on a long trip. Why carry maps of Italy and postcards of Michaelangelo's statues to Sweden by train? Send them by manila.
3. Address your postcards in advance. Type or print the addresses of your friends and relatives on gummed label sheets from the stationery store. Why spend hours leafing through your address book when you could be gazing at the Mona Lisa?
4. Does your hotel have a package-mailing service? Make inquiries. Send home clothes (that you don't need) and souvenirs. Box them up!

MONEY STRATEGIES

1. Make two copies of your credit cards. Leave one copy at home and carry the other with you, separate from the credit cards themselves. If they are lost or stolen, you'll have all of the necessary data.
2. If your trip includes foreign coin accumulations, look for a coin purse with two compartments. It's frustrating when American currency gets mixed up with foreign money.
3. Keep tip money in a readily available spot. Know how much to pay bellboys ahead of time. Avoid last-minute fumbling.
4. For a long trip, an American Express card is a necessity. With it, you can cash personal checks up to one thousand dollars. You'll receive two hundred dollars in cash, the rest in travelers checks.
5. Never fly with your money in your suitcase. Locks are fairly useless and your funds can be easily lost or stolen. Tuck a fifty-dollar bill on your person, in a pocket, money belt, or pinned to your underwear. It can rescue you if your wallet or purse is stolen. Always carry travelers checks rather than cash!

GROOMING, TOILETRIES, ETC.

1. Use midget-sized bottles and jars for shampoos, lotions, and creams. Department and variety stores carry collections of little containers just for travelers. Fill the bottles only three-quarters full to allow for air pressure.
2. Men can trade in their heavy Dopp Kits for lightweight nylon ones. Women, try the dual-compartment toiletry cases made by Trina and Celebrity. Take a separate zippered bag for a mini-blowdryer and styling brush.
3. If you travel often, keep a complete kit of toiletries packed and ready to go, whether for two days or two weeks. You never travel without these items, so keep them handy.
4. Pressurized cabins are dry, dehydrating climates. Pack chapstick, hand lotion, and moisturizer for your face in your carry-on bag. Apply moisturizers several times during a flight. Also, wear very little makeup if you plan to reapply creams. Get pretty just before arrival.
5. Are you going on a trip with your lover? Share unisex toiletries: shampoo, toothpaste, blowdryer, unscented deodorant, hairbrush, and razor. You'll save space.
6. Have you seen those little moist towelettes that come in tiny envelopes? They are often packed and seldom used. Don't bring them unless you are going to a desert. Travel light!

PACKING HINTS

1. Shoes must be covered to protect them from scratches and to keep them from soiling your clothes. Put them in Baggies or old socks. Make drawstrings bags or buy shoe mitts at your local department store.

2. Neckties can be folded over a sturdy piece of cardboard and secured with a rubber band.

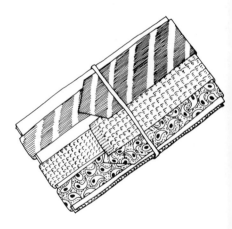

3. Pack one skirt hanger! Most hotels don't have them. Or bring large safety pins and attach your skirts to the hangers the way the dry cleaners do.

4. Packing a skirt or dress inside-out inverts the creases, making them less obvious. It sounds strange, but it works for some people.

5. Cut a piece of grosgrain ribbon and poke tiny pierced earring studs into it. Pack it with your other jewelry in a zippered bag called a jewelry roll, which can be purchased in department stores.

6. Do you want to do laundry in your hotel room? Luggage departments carry thin clotheslines with miniature clothespins. Buy some coin envelopes and fill them with powdered Woolite or your favorite cold water detergent. You can also purchase towelettes of spot remover.

7. Have you seen the "hanging bureau," a hanging bag with five to seven zippered compartments for small items—lingerie, swimwear, nightwear, and socks? I use mine as a dresser in my closet as well as for trips. Hanging bureaus cost about twenty-five dollars.

8. Save your plastic bags from grocery shopping by storing them in your suitcase. Then, when you're ready to go, you'll have all the right-sized bags to pack your clothes in.

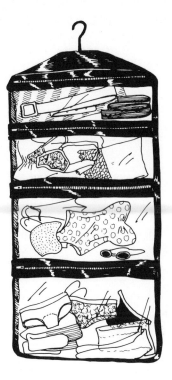

NOTES